Suddenly,
SO MUCH

Suddenly,
SO MUCH

Sandy Shreve

TORONTO

Exile Editions
2005

First published in Canada in 2005 by
Exile Editions Ltd.
20 Dale Avenue
Toronto, Ontario, M4W 1K4
telephone: 416 485 9468
www.ExileEditions.com

Library and Archives Canada Cataloguing in Publication

Shreve, Sandy
    Suddenly, so much / Sandy Shreve.

Poems.
ISBN 1-55096-652-9

    I. Title.

PS8587.H75S83 2005   C811'.54   C2005-905255-4

Design and Composition: Michael P.M. Callaghan
Cover Painting (detail): Gabriela Campos
Typesetting: Moons of Jupiter
Printed in Canada by: Gauvin Imprimerie

The publisher would like to acknowledge the financial assistance of
The Canada Council for the Arts.

THE CANADA COUNCIL | LE CONSEIL DES ARTS
FOR THE ARTS | DU CANADA
SINCE 1957 | DEPUIS 1957

10 9 8 7 6 5 4 3 2 1

for
Bill

CONTENTS

Between the hammers lives on
our heart, as between the teeth
the tongue, which, in spite of all,
still continues to praise.

— RAINER MARIA RILKE

Appalacian Spring (Aaron Copland, 1944)

Because the wars are not over yet, and yet
these notes unfold
                    leaf

and bud in the sun   because this
is what comes of bowing strings and breathing

into reeds and what breaks
the sky
            is dawn not bombs because

a ballet begins with a long sliver of sound
the piano

            laughs, woodwinds scamper in the grass
with violins my fingers
                        sprout green shoots

and my shuttered heart   opens

Tai Chi Variations

Wild Horse Shakes Her Mane

Everyone thought you were broken
in, tamed like that russet mare
standing in the pasture, her calm eye
on a man fixing the fence.

Everyone thought you were living
content within normal borders, but you
leave unnoticed,
wander unharnessed into the first
yellow strands of dawn, hear

distant violins linger over an oboe,
proclaim spring in the Appalachians.

You shed winter from your limbs,
reach into air as if to hold
sound in your open hands,
then give it to the wind again
and follow.

White Crane Spreads Her Wings

She stands at the edge
of a lagoon, still
hunter patiently waiting
for fish, she stands
out, white target in green reeds
where redwings take off,
dive-bomb the idea
of a threat.

You name this moment
white statue in water.

Then the statue opens
each wing like a wave —
you want to learn
all the possibilities
in her elegant strength,
to keep your balance
even under attack
fearlessly
to lift your arms into the air,
expose your heart
without surrender.

Strum the Guitar

All your life you've tried
to synchronize fingers and string,

a fascination that began
tangled in laces and cats' cradles,

the imagined music in a mute guitar
on a cottage wall —

begging your uncle to play,
though an inkling that he'd forgotten

how, crept between his evasions
like betrayal. Years later

you spent hours with the gift
your mother could not afford,

feeling your way into the rhythms
of protest and love. Now you reach

a moment in this sequence
where you can break an opponent's arm

or waltz with what your own two hands
have abandoned, hold

the hope of harmony
in your arms again.

Repulse Monkey

You ease back a step, pass
one palm over the other, reach—

for the cute curly-tailed primate swinging tree to tree
you're supposed to push away. Wonder,
why monkey? Remember

a rigid line of militia in the sixties, those foolish
and beautiful students, watching the visored
eyes of their brothers and sliding
daisies into the muzzles of M16s
as if weapons could be vases.

You'd rather shove the violent
off the face of the earth, but it is
more complicated than that—monkey

is one name for a small
gun, and the delicate mimulus.

You ease back a step,
pass one palm over the other   reach
for a stance of praise.

Grasp the Sparrow's Tail

You want to fly with your feet
anchored to the ground, like bamboo
in the wind

where sparrows congregate,
impatient,
they do not wait
long for another turn at the feeder,
are quick to flap chickadees
away from their seeds.

More like demons
than souls released from the bondage
of our bodies, these birds
flick their little tails,
insolent.

You happily snatch one
down from its ecstasy in sky

and as you pull it back to live
on this earth again,
its heart turns to a terror
your fingers cannot bear to hold.

When you let go,
your feathered hands soar.

Wave Hands like Clouds

Wrapped in an aura of warmth,
your hands cast spells —

frost on the lawn becomes mist
lifting, as if to water the stars, while you

sidle toward a world
you must confront,

decorate daybreak with ribbons of shade
and brilliant light.

Dangerous and playful,
the wide intent of your eyes.

There are no storms in the clouds
you create   but

they will travel far,
little white arias in heaven's blue

eye, they will crescendo
elsewhere to cast lightning and rain

out of a violet sky.

Double Wind Blows in Ears

This is no place for the doldrums,
though at first your palms are flat,
facing out, calling a halt
to extremes, their opposite seasons.

You reel in summer
from the south Pacific, winter
from Arctic lands,
hold them close, believing

you are capable of taming both
monsoons at once,
that your two lungs can contain
all the howling in the world, transform it

to a warm breeze. You think
you've been turning the wind
into kisses,
but your hands are clenched.

For the first time, you know
how to use your fists, discover
you can strike a blow
at the temple of your enemy.

Snake Creeps Down

You start at the end
of a kick to the groin, one arm hooked
high in the air, the other
folded over your heart. Balanced

graceful as a crane
on one leg, you are poised to grab
Jacob's ladder and climb —

but your foot is on the snake's tail
and you must

slide. You think of the snake, not
as gendered, as devil or deity,
but indifferent, the androgynous
arm of a pendulum, bearing
your weight as you swoop
to the ground and rise into air again,

its inevitable arc carrying you
safely home.

Needle at Sea Bottom

In middle-age you begin
to forget little things, lose them
like dropped stitches. Just yesterday,
even the needle disappeared into the depths
where the misplaced wait

to be retrieved. Now you stroke the air
as if you are crawling through water,
but the movement becomes a dive deep enough
to touch bottom.

All the way down you peer into green
light, caress memories you have long wanted
back, gather them into your arms
until it is time to breathe again

and resurface, buoyantly
empty-handed.

Cross Hands

You have crossed your fingers
until the tips were white with hope
or betrayal, crossed

lines, arbitrary and fixed
borders, bridges, even continents,
friends,
your heart.

Here, in the space between
two willows, their canopy
shading the path you've made
of battle and ballet,
you cross your hands
in front of your face

as if to embrace where you stand,
though you've wound up
at the crossroads
in an endless figure eight—

almost the same place
where you began.

Triptych, After Mary Pratt

*Maybe women are turned on by objects, the things
around them. The stuff that women collect speaks
to women and women give it to men.*

—MARY PRATT

For the Love of These Oranges

Something as simple as an orange
exposed.

One curlicue strip
tease of peel, voluptuous

fruit, flamboyant on foil,
chrome light soaked with this

disrobing. Even the crystal goblet
sweats, dazzled with citrus.

Your mouth juices up.

You try to calm yourself,
nestle into the placid background—
maroon infused with phantoms,
a radiant passage—
                            breathe deeply
this warm afterglow to the passion
of oranges.

As if they know communion cannot hold
the tingle, the ache, these
apparitions laugh and dance and clap
when you glance back
to the bright fandangle

on display in a public gallery,

grasp again for the one undressing,
greedily drain the glass and beg
for more.

Glassy Apples

The truth is, the snake had nothing at all to do with it, in fact
was not even a serpent, but a worm poking his little head
out of an apple as Eve passed by

                              gathering food in the orchard
for her wedding and the green maggot wanted an invitation
to the feast. Being a woman,

                    Eve knew all about
buffets, how a table should please the eye first, then the palate,
so she plucked only the finest fruit. Set aside

                              one particular
red delicious, its skin as smooth as her own and Adam's youth,
sliced it open to expose the magic

                              pentacle centre, perfect
brown seeds in a bed white as sheets—for luck and long life as
each bit into half, sealing

                    their marriage vows,
and all in the garden cheered, except the worm who cursed
the whole affair from afar, vowed

                              revenge, thought up
the story of forbidden fruit while he watched the guests gobble
what he wanted:

those gorgeous apples in glass bowls,
on that glass table top she put there on purpose to catch
the glimmer of sun

on his favourite fruit, placed in calm
repose upon a bed of reflections where tongues of light
licked skin, now burnished

to a passion he'd never imagined
possible, and kept where he couldn't get at it. I'll make
them pay for this, he snickered,

gripping his pen
and, knowing a grub was too abhorrent to be believed
even in Paradise,

used snake as pseudonym, named
Eve temptress, Adam sinner, and invented a God
of vengeance; kept his eye

on the glitter of envy and
avarice while he made up shame and never even noticed
at the bottom of it all, left of centre, his own

small heart
bursting with unrequited love.

Red Currant Jelly

How much depends
upon

a child's reach
across

skittishly crinkled
tinfoil

gulping the sky
blue and

ruby luminous
jelly

to dip her finger
into

a bowl brimming
sugar-

thick pink froth
under

the sun's yellow
glare

Illuminares

Footsteps

*At rubbing trees and only at rubbing trees, bears walk in the paw
prints of those who have gone before them.*
— MARK HUME *(River of the Angry Moon)*

How does anyone know whose steps to follow, where
anything, even your own footfall
alone, might lead?

Somewhere in the rain forest,
a quiet, like the moment after a raven laughs,
is falling.

A Douglas fir rises into the silence, exhales
the resin scent of a permanent wound — its ridged bark
worn away by bears

who approach this tree, step
by measured step, sink into a lineage of tracks
the long-since dead laid down,

observe the meticulous ritual,
then scratch their backs. A small thing prefaced with such
reverence, there is

a hint of wonder in this place,
a mysterious ursine way preserved in these huge prints,
as if the bears must honour

those who have gone before,
and choose to do so here instead of there, bowing
their great heads

in a humble dance. Then again,
I have seen two coyotes, north of here and snowbound,
traipse one ahead of the other,

shrugging their shoulders
at the cold as they snuffled white air for otters
near a fishing hole. Almost

without looking, the one behind
placed each paw precisely in the leader's tracks.

Nothing

to it. Heel, toe. See?

This way.

Evergreen

The cedar wags its ragged crown,
limbs thrashing at the mountain
out of reach—
as if, before it was a tree
it strolled those slopes on four furred paws,
daily raised them up, claws
unsheathed, to shred the very bark it would
become—
a green bear howling for its former home.

Lament

Beyond a borderline of grass, and past
lilies of the valley huddled underneath the fallen
needles of the spruce and hemlock,

someone cut the brambles down.

Just yesterday, this space was air designed
for chaos, archways thick with leaves and warblers,
an untamed strip of land along a public path.

Perhaps some passerby complained

of wayward branches, thorns attacking ankles, or
an eyesore— saw weeds and wildness where
more properly a city lawn should front the trees.

The ground is stiff and stubbled now

and without song
starlings poke their beaks at broken branches.
The unrestrained has met the blade.

Today, November rain.

Blink

The gopher owns this prairie
moonlight on the grass —
invisible, the harrier

Disappeared

A piece of pizza on the table.
Half a glass of coke.

She'd just moved to the city
Nervous but determined.

Her clothes
For the morning shift laid out.

Only half an hour away.
A movie played ten minutes. Put on hold. No sign

Of struggle. Headlines guessing
While the sludge along the Memramcook sucked
Week after week the searchers' boots.

Her boyfriend wept, denied denied denied.
We sat at home imagining
The worst things. Until we told ourselves

Not to hope, told ourselves   of all the possibilities
Only death had mercy. Imagined all

The worst things   except
The worst   what they found.

At least we know, we tell ourselves at least
We know.   God help us, what they found.

Most days, we can't say it
Out loud.

Fog

Misty-eyed morning —
what's left of the moon dissolves.
Somewhere, the rains rain

Adieu

There is not much time. The birds sing of winter
though the leaves light up the air with their dying.
Sumachs scorch their fingers, burn at the end to hail
heaven where poplars

drizzle down from their great green heights to the ground
wearing gold, a last fling with the brilliant
chill. Is this praise or defiance; is it God
or the coffin

that leaves us trembling when we drift away
from the gravestones and the unknown:—how long do we have;
are the dead we mourn part of the song or are they
simply gone

Crows

*Romans regarded the crow as a symbol of the future
because it cries* Cras, cras *(Tomorrow, tomorrow).*
—BARBARA G. WALKER

Out of all four corners of the world,
these ancients with tomorrow on their tongues
gather one by one,

cackle from whatever throne
they find to occupy—
at the edges of our eyes, the crows'

feet etch our every smile,
as if the only thing in life that matters
is our laughter.

Creatures of both earth and sky, they do not
care if we believe them evil,
dread them as death's messengers

or simply scorn them for the mess they make
scavenging through garbage in the park.
Always dressed for funerals,

crows know they are the pallbearers for our souls,
their gift, to find the glitter in what we leave behind.

Arachne

The points of leaves and twigs on which the Spider begins her
work are few, And she fills the Air with a beautiful circuiting.
—JOHN KEATS

The points of leaves and twigs are thick
with new green, sprouting from the apple tree,

the lilac hedge and firs—the options,
like spring promises, abundant. But those

on which the spider begins her work
are few, anchoring the barricade

she builds around our house, every night
weaves shutters on each window, laces up the doors,

drapes another tapestry across the porch.
And she fills the air with a hunter's patience

knowing, come the dawn we will emerge
wielding sticks, and she will have to spin

a beautiful circuiting again.
While we dream, she feasts on what she can,

leaves skeletons like trophies
dangling from her intricate designs—

or are they warnings?

The Eleventh Situation

*Gozzi maintained that there can be but thirty-six tragic situations.
Schiller took great pains to find more, but he was unable to find
even so many as Gozzi.*

—GOETHE

Another enigma. You're drawn in again, tempted
again to convict the obvious suspect without question.
Except it doesn't work. The lover's alibi,
clearly designed to beguile anyone looking
into his whereabouts, holds up. You assume the problem
lies elsewhere, begin to search for a subliminal hint

lurking in the kitchen. Surely this is where such a hint
would take shape. Bare counters. Cold stove. You're tempted
by aromas, follow them outdoors where a minor problem
takes your mind off the all-important question.
A small voice you ignore tries to suggest you've overlooked
something. You're too busy sniffing two intricate alibis,

morning glory and roses, hopelessly intertwined. Alibi
four steps forward, obsessively dissembling, hints
she likes roses too. You lose track of what you were looking
for, wander back inside where you try tempting
the husband with incriminating questions.
His answers implicate the maid who was away. The problem

seems to be your inability to solve problems.
Stonewalled by everyone, even the most obtuse alibi
secure, you suspect you never knew how to question
suspects. In the corner of your eye a new hint
ducks in and out of the garage (perhaps you can tempt
the chauffeur with a trap) but the camera is looking

at the victim's sister watching the game and you're looking
at third strike for the third time. Face it, the problem
was out of control the minute you forgot that temptation
involves deceit. Was it really a perfect alibi
that led you astray? Did you imagine every hint?
You're not quite ready to question

your own motives — if you start that line of questioning
there'll be no end to it and you're out of time as it looks
like the end is near. At last an obscure hint
surfaces, explaining nuances until the problem
dissolves and the case is cracked with a broken alibi
(finally!). The small voice interrupts when the ads attempt

to tempt you with mattress sales and a barbecue hinting
at your hunger. It says the only problem worth looking
into is all you will buy without question.

Hearts

She plays the game with grace, although at first
it frightened her—the room, the smoke, the thirst
    to take control before her heart was broken
    by the rules of chance, whims written
in a careless hand the gods cursed

and left for fools. She's learned the best and worst
come and go; deals the deck, immersed
    in all-or-nothing tricks, eyes watchful when
                  she plays. The game

goes on and on. The reckless bet their shirts
on nothing much, wearing hopes and hurts
    thin; she feigns indifference—lands unbidden
    on a fickle diamond. She is the queen
sought and shunned, who shuffles luck's reversals—
                  she plays the game.

Landing

What you see is what you get
to come home to. Flickering in the night,
the city flirts with its own shadow, charms
what you see. Is what you'll get
drawn into the front porch lit with someone
waiting eagerly, or a darkened door?
What you see, is. What you get
to come home to flickers in the night.

Passion

*A glass-blower, remember, breathes life into a vessel, giving it
shape and form and sometimes beauty; but he can with that
same breath, shatter and destroy it.*
     —DAPHNE DUMAURIER *(The Glass Blowers)*

You arrange my red glads
and dahlias   passion

in a glass vase.

Everything in this room
is fragile.

We made it that way, one loving
breath at a time   best

friends,
husband, wife.

               After all these years,
draw lines

straight and tentative as cut stems:
If it comes to this   or this

I will leave you, leave
good enough
               alone,

depending. Is this enough?

Is even asking
               too much?

The Scroll

Everything I should have said, and didn't.
Everything: 'I should'.
Have said, and didn't everything…
I should have said "and."
Didn't everything?
I should have said!
And didn't. Everything.

Vesper

— for Claire Meggs

White plum blossoms shiver to our garden,
tiny votive candles lit against another

dark, the wind at rest in cedars and the hour
cathedral quiet.
                    Air

after rain. As if the world has paused,
and the pause, anticipation. Shadows stand

aside for praise, a cello air, the solo aching
in the rise and fall of a heart
                                        beat.

Midnight, Again

Rain music on leaves —
night creatures munching, run off
their little wet feet.

Guardian

Hope sways with the heron on a black bough
gone wild—the storm sleepless, trying
to pitch them from their nest into the night
like brittle wings clipped and dumped with the rest
of the dead, the broken and fallen crushing mauve
primrose and hyacinth; faith fading to darkness
as bleak as the back of the moon where nightmares menace
unfettered by a lucid dawn, gentle
breeze or daydream. Yet the heron on a black
bough gone wild in a wind storm, sleepless
throughout the night, faced with the rest of the dead,
the broken and fallen, the crushed primrose and hyacinth
at the edge of a bleak and moonless future filled
with a nightmare menace unfettered by dawn's lucid
tread, gentle breeze or daydream—regains
his precarious balance, holding on to hope.

Sunrise

Night flings itself back,
spins into brilliance
for a moment
concrete is gold, and glass, fire.

Darling Illusions

A prism in the window, spinning daydreams
fall across the floor, all afternoon
in this room—the window open to a time
when we didn't care about the world

breaking in; one spring when I sat laughing
at the cat for chasing rainbows

Walls

> *Something there is that doesn't love a wall*
> *That wants it down.*
> > —Robert Frost ("Mending Wall")

Day and night the timbers creak, withstanding
wind, the clash of outer cold and inner
heat. They groan from years of standing here
without their wandering roots, stripped bare of leaves

and branches, stripped of bark. The human love
and need for wood admires the inner grain
flattened into planks and soaked with varathane
instead of sap, the swirl of years preserved

within a wall. Outside, the living firs
lift restless air, with outstretched arms caress
their shorn and fallen cousins, transformed to shelter
for our breathing. Perhaps it's only breath

and wind in some precarious balance that keeps
these walls upright. A house inhabited
might list a bit with age upon foundations
sinking into soil, but once abandoned,

it's as if there's nothing left for walls
to stand for—no paintings left to hold up
to an eye, no couch or chair or desk to
rest against. There's no one home to renovate

and mend, no one to trust, except the something
that doesn't love a wall,

                      that wants it down.

Field

Clover vetch and devil's paintbrush
dandelion and chamomile
violets snapdragons butter & eggs
the bluebell the lupin the Queen Anne's lace
a yarrow a buttercup a thistle a daisy
grasshoppers garter-snakes bees
and me

Back Roads

are supposed to be
a way of going nowhere

special after Sunday services or picnics,
the slow drive home along the Aboujagane

dodging hunters' guns; the way we take
for granted family stories, always the same

turn toward expected places, an echo
of the car horn tooting through the covered bridge,

a few stray details pinging
at the oil pan as we pass the graveyard,

our ghosts in dust-balloons behind
bald tires, a kind of camouflage we know

by heart where the potholes are, how
to get around them and

how not to.

Revisiting Chance and Change

Yet will I stay my steps and not go down to the marshland, —
Muse and recall far off, rather remember than see, —
Lest on too close sight I miss the darling illusion,
Spy at their task even here the hands of chance and change.
— SIR CHARLES G.D. ROBERTS
("Tantramar Revisited," *1886*)

Odd, how the hands that held you back are the ones
that draw me near, urging me into a landscape you

would think ruined, bleached pylons rising
in reeds by the dyke where I watch for herons — blue

beacons guarding the sullen decay of wharves, forsaken
when the tides altered course. An island was born,

left you hesitating on the hill, yet bequeathed to me
this rhythm of the Tantramar.

We greet changes to childhood haunts
awkwardly, want home to stand still while we

wander off making strangers
of ourselves, hoping for the familiar

when we return — marsh hawks still tipping
their wings to the few grey barns that remain,

beams sagging into an old scent of cedar and hay.
It's more than a hundred years since you kept

your distance but the river
keeps rushing in with the wind nipping at cattails,

the mud flats are as red as ever—and there
is the place I imagined myself

tucked inside a redwing's solitary call. The ground
is under water now, restored to wetlands—

                                        Listen

the bobolink is back

Illuminares

In my bestiary of extinctions, hope,
earth's angel, is a heron.

—Don McKay
("Sunday Morning, Raisin River")

What happened here last night is done
and the heron's gone.

For now, coots and mallards hug
the reeds, preen while yellow irises invade the north
lagoon, where a stranger placed
his lantern in the water—a winking invitation

to the multitude. They came
from Kitsilano, Point Grey and the suburbs, shaped
imagination with their breath inside balloons
and papier mâché:

          Dumbo, Eeyore, Tigger, welcome
back, to hang

from makeshift fishing rods, bait
the night with an inner light and catch
the clamour of conflicting drums and tambourines,

a frenzy of mosquitoes
          feeding,
shouts and chaos drowning out Ukrainian women
singing in the willow grove, an alto sax grieving

for the years when only neighbours came, when there was
space to promenade around this lake behind a prancing
dragon, pause beside each boardwalk, each small wharf
a stage for dancers or musicians, and the air
a soft applause

                    an absence undetected by this crowd
of thousands, drawn irresistibly to our east-end park,
the rumours of community.

When will the heron
                  come back here to greet
the dawn, hunt and spend the night?
                       Soon

I'll wander home, the little league will fill
the baseball fields and families will arrive
for Sunday barbecues. From my porch,
I'll listen for familiar voices lifting,
            falling,
lifting, in the wake of great blue wings.

                 — *Trout Lake, Vancouver, 1999*

Sidelines

How we adore the flamboyant—feisty red,
burnt orange, gold. We cheer them
on from the sidelines, waving, taking
pictures, shouting their names
with *hurray! hurray!* ... and a bit of envy,
though we know there is much to be

said for the ones going out in their dowdy
dresses, ochres and browns old-
fashioned and eloquent; something about
their dignified lives that makes us want to sit
down in a small parlour, sip
tea, exchange recipes.

Suddenly there is so much to celebrate, so little
time before the rains arrive, and the wind

Essence

Beauty is in the eye of the beholder.
Even a dull October day lifts the spirit
who loves rain. Even grey, if grey
beauty is in the eye. Of the beholder
drenched in essence of mist, it is said she
laughs at the ghost of sorrow, lost in what
beauty is. In the eye of the beholder —
even a dull October day. The spirit lifts.

Today, a Cormorant

Is a beautiful black bird
watching us through emerald eyes?

While he hangs his wings out to dry
he is jiggling a little wet from his feathers,
as if to tease or dare. He bares his breast
in this park where we unleash our dogs.
Seems he flew in from the coast and
decided to fish in the city for a change,

dropped by our lake just
today, a cormorant
dropped by our lake, just

decided to fish in the city for a change.
Seems he flew in from the coast, and
in this park (where we unleash our dogs)
as if to tease or dare—he bares his breast.
He is jiggling a little wet from his feathers
while he hangs his wings out to dry.

Watching us through emerald eyes
is a beautiful black bird.

Autumn Pantoum

Each quick appearance is a farewell—
the leaves blush and wave goodbye;
goodbye, goodbye to green, everything
eventually dies.

The leaves blush and wave goodbye,
even the junco trilling hello
eventually dies
down, rejoicing becomes requiem.

Even the junco trilling 'hello
cold' is a sign of beginning, of winter coming
down. Rejoicing becomes requiem.
This small bird sings for angels and ghosts.

Cold is a sign of beginning, of winter coming
with white ideas of ice and snow.
This small bird sings for angels and ghosts
rummaging at dusk under a grove of oaks.

With white ideas of ice and snow,
mallards abandon the lake and rushes
to rummage at dusk under a grove of oaks,
butting their beaks at the leaves. They mutter.

Mallards abandon the lake and rushes—
I hear them after dark when they should be asleep,
butting their beaks at the leaves. They mutter
goodbye at last. Listen,

I hear them after dark when they should be asleep.
Goodbye. Goodbye to green. Everything,
goodbye at last. Listen —
each quick appearance is a farewell.

Elles

"In 1894, Lautrec took up residence at the brothel on the rue des Moulins, where he produced many drawings and paintings of the women of the house as they relaxed, slept or were otherwise uninvolved in their profession. The 1896 Elles series of lithographs is the final result of this prolonged visit and is the artist's most eloquent homage to the women of the rue des Moulins and others of their profession."

—Phillip Dennis Cate

Frontispiece

I could be taking down my hair; could be
about to pin it up.
                        In my blue
dressing gown, I have perhaps just
come home, or am getting ready
to go out. Either way,
a lovely bonnet and a man's top hat
wait on the bed.

When I was small, the city was a rumour
passing through our village. Always, I intended
to shrug the Cévennes off my back.
A restless thoroughbred,

                        I would fix my red
hair in the fashion of fine ladies, turn
pirouettes at the roadside
when gentlemen in their carriages
drove by —

            I used to dream of Paris
and wild horses.

The Seated Clowness—Mademoiselle Cha-u-ka-o

For sure, I can act. Put me in a costume
and voila! I am a gorgeous acrobat.
Even the bourgeois women let go of their
        rosaries to clap.

(*Calice*, this vulgar collar...) They have great fun
at the Moulin Rouge (the cut's low, the yellow
loud) pretending they are not who they are. See
        how they drift across—

Can you picture me slouched like this, spreading my
legs in their parlours? The best seat in the house
tonight is here, away from their grins. Tonight,
        I am tired of them.

Woman with a Tray—Breakfast
Madame Baron and Mademoiselle Popo

Is this the way she will
remember me? A mother with her back turned
to her daughter —

            I would take her
away from here if I could. Perhaps
if I had abandoned
her at birth…

            Now all I can do is take away
the tray, worry about her
inadequate breakfast, coffee
with a bit of cream. She watches

me leave, is still in bed, reclining
on her side, hair
tousled, head propped
in her hand. Where on earth did he find

all that love in her eyes?

Sleeping Woman—Awakening

Such luxury, to be alone
in my bed:

      when morning slips
her finger between the curtains

I never open my eyes
willingly—all night the feather pillows

and down quilts
hold me in their memory of wings

Woman at the Tub–The Tub

I keep an etching of Leda
and the Swan on my wall, the bust
of a monocled man on the mantle.

They seem to put my well-dressed
customers at ease
                              and they do amuse
with their mythologies.

Ah, pardonnez-moi — I forget
that to mention this
is distracting. You are meant to see me
fully dressed

in front of the fire, bending over
my bath and testing
the water.

Woman Washing Herself—The Toilette

When you think about it, really it is odd
the way we choose one part
of the body
        to love best. How we

bargain with God over tragedies
that may never happen —

*take an arm if you must, but leave me
two good legs;
        my hearing
but never my sight*

        This young artist
loves women's backs. While he was drawing
mine, I asked him to put down
his crayon, and wash that bit in the middle
I almost can't reach.

        Me, I adore
breasts, and the way you get a glimpse
of mine, full and firm in the small
mirror above the wash basin
is my favourite part of this picture.

Woman with Mirror—The Hand Mirror

For now we see through a glass darkly; but then face to face:
now I know in part; but then shall I know even as also I am known.
—1 CORINTHIANS 13.12

He has shaded in most of my looking glass
with a messy cross-hatch. All

you can see of my reflection is a corner
of my forehead, one eye and
a high cheekbone; a tuft of unruly hair.

A bit literal.

        I don't much care
for the way he has my night dress torn
and falling off my right shoulder, or how
my robe is tossed carelessly across
that chair. Even though my bed is

made and my yellow slippers shout "tidy"
from the floor—I and my room
look used.

Still, he put me
in the foreground taking up a lot
of space and standing
tall, the way my mother taught me.

Sandy Shreve

You ask what I'm thinking as I gaze
into my mirror. Notice

the comb in my hand.

Woman Combing Her Hair–The Coiffure

I sit on the floor
alone, in my darkened room—
dream of sunflowers,
eyes on the ground, looking much
like mine; the wind in their hair.

Woman in Bed, Profile–Awakening

Well now, would you look at us. Two whores
in the morning. Who cares? That was my
first reaction, seeing me sitting up in bed (my sheets
and velvet coverlet so neat you'd think I'd hardly
slept a wink) and Eloise standing by
like any young girl's guardian.

Even so, I wish I were less rigid in this picture. I seem
slightly peeved, a little sullen. Eloise, she's all
warmth and kindness, as if she's being
patient with me. I was told

it's all about how my squandered youth has nothing
to look forward to but Eloise's sagging shape and
undesired age. So, this afternoon while we were playing
cards, I asked him. Henri, I said, since when
was getting old unique to prostitutes? He poured
us both another drink. Then grinned
and raised his glass to me.

Woman in Her Corset—Passing Conquest

Uncanny, how so many
men
    like to watch
me dress. This one, bow-tied,

tucked into his hat and tails
is especially fond
of my corsets. He
        sits
like an obedient child.

He will not lift his gloved hand
to help me.

Reclining Woman—Weariness

I suppose I ought to get up,
get going—
        take off my other sock,
comb my hair, box my hat, hang
up my pretty gown, maybe

clean this room. Just
           give me

one minute more
to stare at the ceiling as if it were
blue sky, and my bed
           an open pasture

while I rest my head in my hands.

Whisper Songs

Whisper Songs

...there is a phenomenon called the "whisper song" in which the bird sings almost inaudibly, as though in the back of its throat, so quietly that one must be very close in order to hear it.

— JOHN A. LIVINGSTON (*Rogue Primate*)

1.

An ordinary draft disturbs the curtain,
lets morning whisper in, a brief surprise —
sunlight wavers, then goes out again,

a candle snuffed, another shuttered eye
and day descends weighted with regret.
More cloud, more cold; rain turns to flurries

turn to rain — even the weather forgets
what it's supposed to do. Voices scramble
into the room, the news a breakfast of threats

I wish I could ignore. Listen to the babble
and destruction pouring in, the gossip and thunder,
the conviction. I'd rather sweet nothings — fragile

vows, nonsense words, the lust of love-birds,
the hustle of buds bursting the seams of winter.

2.

The hustle of buds bursting the seams of winter,
a dream away—these days reluctant stubs
of their summer selves. Chimney-smoke lingers,

the air sweet-scented with indifference. A mob
flaps at the feeder, another squabble in the chill
drags on. (What whisper songs?) Seeds like crumbs

from the table of unlikely gods are trampled and spill,
attracting mice—and mice find all the flaws
in our foundation. We poison them. A little

life is taken just because it crawled
to us for shelter—and we are not ashamed,
refill the feeder because we want to be awed

by finches and chickadees, their antics, the untamed
feasting outside our window, unafraid.

3.

Feasting outside our window, unafraid
though a merlin lives nearby, sparrows festoon
the bamboo, preen their muted plumage and wait

their turn the way we wait for change. In the woods
sap begins to run, a sure sign. Spring thaw
always starts with a trickle. It dawdles, then pools

in our hearts, hope tiptoeing in to sprawl
on the couch — an old friend who never left.
When the cold snap comes hope fades as fast as the hawk

snatches food. Somehow I never expect
a varied thrush in its talons. From the brambles, a clamour
in the key of grief, a slight shudder when the breath-

less wind settles. Hidden in Douglas firs
a flicker clings to the bark and starts to hammer.

4.

A flicker clings to the bark and starts to hammer
in a language we think we understand. The tempo
insists we listen again, dares us to measure

the space between each beat, imagine echoes
that live there. Out of the shadows, a coyote appears,
a grey hesitation. She holds something in her yellow

stare, poised on the periphery where need meets fear
and contemplates. The flicker changes his tune
to laughter — the song, a haunted mockery piercing

the air, mocking the coyote's indecision
or mocking mine. Then the coyote, in one smooth leap,
leaps over thorns into the afternoon.

Above the garden long since gone to seed,
overcast hours drift on, seamlessly.

5.

Overcast hours drift on, seamlessly
shifting tenses. A wayward breath is intent
on shaking loose the silver gleam we see

in the drop that clings to a leaf—the not yet
and the irrepressible now. The wait for a wish
almost granted; the song in a whispered moment

almost heard. Perhaps I've grown deaf to riffs
floating over my head, euphonious hymns
from a world beyond my eager reach, my stiff

wings. Far off, two bald eagles hem
a ragged cloud, then ride thermals—feather
and wind, adrift and dreaming, carry them

into the infinite. When they return they offer
no answer, only an elegant will to endure.

6.

No answer. Only an elegant will to endure
where anything can happen (and soon). We know
too much and too little to rely on gestures

toward faith we keep making. (A prayer said, *sotto
voce*, against aggression; then after it happens,
the vigil, a crowd gathered in darkness, holding

hands and candles.) A wing-beat before sundown,
the feral world around me seems to retreat
in the last light, a quiet so intimate even

rooks rephrase their accusations, their bleak
prophecies—though the roost is in the crosshairs
of survey crews and planners. Who will speak

up for troublesome crows, when all across
the city, rush hour idles at the crossroads...

7.

City rush hour idles at the crossroads,
a grey hesitation filled with echoes, imagined
and real, incantations from restless shadows

where a coyote stands in the rain. As night beckons
to fragile, *sotto voce* vows, a delicate
light wavers around neglected questions

in the irrepressible now. In the not yet,
an eagle and hawk drift toward spring thaw
while unlikely gods pause to contemplate

the reluctant heart — how it can still be awed
watching sparrows feast, undeterred.
Bursting through seams of indifference, today at dawn

a whispered song was sung (and almost heard) when
an ordinary draft disturbed the curtain.

NOTES

Opening Epigraph; The epigraph is from the "Ninth Elegy" of Rainer Maria Rilke's "The Duino Elegies" (trans. J.B. Leishman).

Tai Chi Variations: "The same techniques that were capable of developing internal power for combat also proved to be effective as life prolonging, healing and rejuvenating exercises."—*A Guide to Taijiquan*, by Master Liang Shou-Yu and Wu Wen-Ching (Yang's Marshall Arts Association, 1993, p. 1). Each poem's title is taken from the name of a Tai Chi posture.

Triptych After Mary Pratt: The epigraph is a Mary Pratt quote from "The Substance of Light" exhibition, Vancouver Art Gallery, 1996. Each poem is titled after a Mary Pratt painting.

"Glassy Apples"—"At Gypsy weddings it was customary for the bride and groom to cut the apple, revealing its pentacle, and eat half apiece. Such marriage customs may suggest the real story behind Eve's sharing of an apple with her spouse." —Barbara G. Walker, *The Woman's Dictionary of Symbols and Sacred Objects* (Harper & Rowe, 1988 p. 480).

"Red Currant Jelly"—The opening two lines of this poem are a slight variation of the opening lines of William Carlos Williams' "The Red Wheelbarrow."

Adieu: The poem begins with a line by Patrick Lane (from "Little Birds" in *Too Spare, Too Fierce*).

Crows: The epigraph is from *The Woman's Dictionary of Symbols and Sacred Objects*, by Barbara G. Walker (Harper & Rowe, 1988 p. 398).

Arachne: Keats' line is from a letter to John Hamilton Reynolds, Feb. 19, 1818, quoted in the *Norton Introduction to Poetry*, 2nd edition, 1973, p. 262.

Vesper: After Bach's *Air* from "Suite No. 3 in D for Orchestra"

Darling Illusions: The title is taken from Sir Charles G. D. Roberts' poem, "Tantramar Revisited."

Revisiting Chance and Change: The Tantramar Marsh is a saltwater tidal marsh on the Chignecto Isthmus between New Brunswick and Nova Scotia. The Tantramar River runs through the marsh and rises and falls with the Bay of Fundy tides.

Illuminares: The *Illuminares*, an annual lantern celebration at Trout Lake, a park in Vancouver's east-side, started out as a community event attended by a few hundred people, then grew to attract some 15,000.

Autumn Pantoum: The poem begins and ends with a line by George Bowering (from "Elegy 10" in *Kerrisdale Elegies*).

Elles: These poems were inspired by Henri de Toulouse-Lautrec's *Elles* series of lithographs, and are titled after each of the frontispiece and ten colour plates. The epigraph is from Cate's essay "'Parades,' Paris and Prostitutes," in *Toulouse-Lautrec, The Baldwin M. Collection* (San Diego Museum of Art, 1998 p. 36). The italicized lines at the end of "Frontispiece" are by Leona Gom, from her poem "Secretary Morning."

Acknowledgements

Some of these poems were first published in the following: *Atlantis, The Antigonish Review, Arc, Canadian Literature, CV2, ∂ANDelion, event, Exile, The Fiddlehead, Grain, In Fine Form: The Canadian Anthology of Form Poems* (Polestar, 2005), *The Malahat Review, Matrix, The New Quarterly, Prism International, Pottersfield Portfolio, TickleAce, The Fed Anthology* (Anvil Press, 2003) and *Landmarks* (The Acorn Press, 2001). (See details, below.)

The poems from "Elles" published in *Prism* were awarded the 2001 Earle Birney Prize for Poetry and received a National Magazine Awards honourable mention for poetry (2000); an earlier version of "Tai Chi Variations" was a finalist for the 1999 Malahat Long Poem Prize.

"For the Love of These Oranges" appeared in *Octavo* and excerpted in *Vernissage* and *Nature Rearranged* (Stephen D. Borys, National Gallery of Canada catalogue for "Still Lifes" show); "Crows" and "For the Love of These Oranges" appeared in *The Edges of Time* (Seraphim Editions, 1999); "Wild Horse Shakes Her Mane" appeared in *Elements of English 11* (Harcourt Brace, 2001); "Footsteps" appeared in the anthology *The Wayward Coast* (Far Field Press, 2002); "Autumn Pantoum" appeared in the anthology *Companions and Horizons* (West Coast Line, SFU, 2005).

Atlantis: "For the Love of these Oranges"
The Antigonish Review: "Passion," "Today, A Cormorant" (under the title "Autumn Song")
Arc: "Footsteps," "Arachne"
"Autumn Pantoum" appeared in *Companions and Horizons* (ed., Steve Collis, West Coast Line, 2005)
Canadian Literature: "Grasp the Sparrow's Tail"
CV2: "Red Currant Jelly"
∂ANDelion: "Walls," "Back Roads," "The Scroll"

event: "Disappeared," "Illuminares"

Exile, The Literary Quarterly: "White Crane Spreads Her Wings," "Wave Hands Like Clouds," "Guardian," "Evergreen," "Essence"

The Fed Anthology: "Double Wind Blows in Ears"

The Fiddlehead: "Wild Horse Shakes Her Mane," "Snake Creeps Down," "Whisper Songs" (#s 2, 3, 4, 5)

Grain: "Repulse Monkey"

Landmarks: "Revisiting Chance and Change"

In Fine Form: Landing"

The Malahat Review: "Woman With A Tray — Breakfast," "Reclining Woman — Weariness"; "Autumn Pantoum"

Matrix: "Glassy Apples"

The New Quarterly: "Hearts" *(Summer 2005)*

Prism International: "Woman Washing Herself — The Toilette," "Woman with Mirror — The Hand Mirror," "Woman Combing Her Hair — The Coiffure," Woman in Bed, Profile — Awakening," "Woman in Her Corset — Passing Conquest."

Pottersfield Portfolio: "Appalachian Spring"

TickleAce: "Crows"

About the Author

Suddenly, So Much is Sandy Shreve's fourth poetry collection. Her previous books are *Belonging* (Sono Nis Press, 1997, short-listed for the Milton Acorn People's Poetry Award); *Bewildered Rituals* (Polestar, 1992); and *The Speed of the Wheel Is Up to the Potter* (Quarry Press, 1990).

She co-edited (with Kate Braid) *In Fine Form — The Canadian Book of Form Poetry* (Polestar 2005). Sandy also edited *Working for a Living*, a collection of poems and stories by women about their work. In the 1990s, she founded, and for the first three years co-ordinated, Poetry In Transit, a project that displays poems in SkyTrain cars and buses throughout BC.

Born in Matane, Quebec, Sandy was raised in Sackville, New Brunswick, and now lives in Vancouver, BC. She received her BA in Canadian History from the University of New Brunswick and is currently the Communications Officer for the Legal Services Society. Previously she spent eight years as Departmental Assistant for the Women's Studies Department at Simon Fraser University. She has also worked as a reporter, library assistant, and secretary.